Charles Rogers

Memorials of the Scottish House of Gourlay

Vol. 1

Charles Rogers

Memorials of the Scottish House of Gourlay
Vol. 1

ISBN/EAN: 9783337243852

Printed in Europe, USA, Canada, Australia, Japan

Cover: Foto ©ninafisch / pixelio.de

More available books at **www.hansebooks.com**

Memorials

OF THE

Scottish House of Gourlay

BY THE

Rev. Charles Rogers, D.D., LL.D.

FELLOW OF THE SOCIETY OF ANTIQUARIES OF SCOTLAND; OF THE
ROYAL SOCIETY OF NORTHERN ANTIQUARIES, COPENHAGEN; OF THE
ROYAL SOCIETY OF BOHEMIA, AND OF THE ROYAL HERALDIC SOCIETY
OF ITALY; ASSOCIATE OF THE IMPERIAL ARCHÆOLOGICAL SOCIETY
OF RUSSIA; AND CORRESPONDING MEMBER OF THE HISTORICAL
SOCIETY OF BERLIN; OF THE ROYAL SOCIETY OF TASMANIA, AND
OF THE HISTORICAL AND GENEALOGICAL SOCIETY OF NEW ENGLAND

Edinburgh

PRIVATELY PRINTED

MDCCCLXXXVIII

PREFATORY NOTE.

These " Memorials of the Scottish House of Gourlay " I have been enabled to produce, consequent on the cost of research having been defrayed by an honoured member of the sept. The inquiry has been conducted amply, and it is to be hoped that the result will prove interesting not only to the members of the Family, but also to those concerned in genealogical studies.

CHARLES ROGERS.

EDINBURGH, 6 BARNTON TERRACE,
July 1888.

CONTENTS.

MEMORIALS

OF THE

SCOTTISH HOUSE OF GOURLAY.

Families in the Southern Counties.

DURING the sixteenth century the family of Gourlay held the lands of Sutton Grange in Yorkshire; they also had possessions in Cumberland. William Gourlay of Sutton Grange, who was living about 1588, is described as "a valiant captain in sundry martial services both at home and abroad."[1]

During the twelfth century, the family effected a settlement in Scotland. Ingelram de Gurley is described as having accompanied William the Lion when that king in 1174 returned from his captivity in England. From King William he received lands in Lothian and Clydesdale.[2] He had a son Hugh, who in 1180 is a witness to a grant by Ingelram de Baliol to the Abbey of Arbroath.[3] Hugh de Gurley possessed lands in the Lothians, also in Fife.[4]

[1] Foster's Visitations of Yorkshire, 168.
[2] Howe's History of England, p. 153.
[3] Register of Aberbrothoc, 39.
[4] Chartulary of Newbottle.

B

Ingelram de Gurley witnessed various charters during the reign of Alexander II. (1214-1249). He is one of four witnesses to a charter by which Sybald, son of Walter, grants to the monks of Cupar certain rents of the Mill of Lundyn; the charter is undated, but is in the register followed by another dated in 1220.[1] As "Ingeram de Gurle" he is witness to a charter by which Alan, constable of Lammermoor, grants to the church of Melrose a right of pasture.[2] In 1245 Ingelram de Gurley witnesses a grant by Hew of Malhewe to Thomas de Ross of the lands of Ross of Milnetor, Hallingshaw, and Bathstruth in Angus.[3]

Among those who in 1296 did homage to Edward I. were Matthew de Gurle, whose locality is not given; Roger Gourlay and William de Gourlay, of the county of Edinburgh; William de Gourlay of Balgally in Forfarshire; and Adam de Gourlay, of the county of Roxburgh.[4] On the 2d January 1303-4, Adam de Gourlay the homager, also Alan de Gourlay, were members of a jury appointed by Edward I. to determine as to the succession to Sir Thomas de Chartres, who owned lands in the barony of Wilton, and had died in the year preceding at enmity with the King.[5]

In a mandate, dated 2d September 1296, whereby lands and goods are restored to certain ecclesiastical

[1] Rental Book of Abbey of Cupar, I., 342.

[2] Chartulary of Melrose.

[3] Register of Aberbrothoc, 338.

[4] Ragman Roll.

[5] Exchequer Q.R. Miscellanea, placita, etc., No. 46.

persons, is named Patrick of Gurleghe, parson of the church of Loghorward, in the shire of Edinburgh.[1]

On the 23d December 1292, Edward I., as overlord of the Kingdom of Scotland, intimated to William de Soulis, envoy from Scotland, his remission to William de Lamberton of a fine of ten merks, in which he was amerced by an assize, at the instance of Hugh de Gurlay, in reference to a tenement in Linton.[2] Hugh de Gurlay was, on the 24th May 1297, invited by Edward I., along with the young Earl of Carrick, afterwards King Robert I., and James the Steward of Scotland, and many others, to accompany him in his proposed expedition to Flanders.[3] In the account rendered by Robert Peebles, Chamberlain of Scotland, in 1328, there is included a payment of one hundred shillings to Hugh de Gurlay, by the King's mandate, for a certain old debt.[4]

On the 24th July 1314, Edward II. granted at York, under his own Privy Seal, protections and safe conducts to John de Gourlay and Symon de Gourlay, who were about to proceed to France, along with William de Umfraville, in quest of money for the ransom of Sir Ingelram de Umfraville, a prisoner with the Scots.[5] Sir Ingelram was probably made captive at the battle of Bannockburn.

On the 30th March 1359, Patrick Gourlay, bailie of

---

[1] Rotuli Scotiæ, vol. i., 25, 26.
[2] *Ibid.*, 14⁶.
[3] Close Roll, 25 Edward I., m. 27.

[4] Exchequer Rolls, vol. i., 216.
[5] Privy Seals (Tower), 8 Edward II., file 4.

Haddington, rendered to the Chamberlain at Dundee his account for that burgh.[1]

On the 26th October 1365, " John Gourlay, merchant of Scotland," received permission to enter England with four companions ; and at the same date William Gourlay, " merchant of Scotland," with four companions, had a similar licence.[2]

In August 1534, Mr Norman Gourlay, apparently a native of the Lothians, was, along with David Stratoun, of the house of Lauriston, charged with heresy in the Abbey Church of Holyrood. At the trial, James V., then in his twenty-second year, was present, clothed in red. Condemned to perish at the stake, the prisoners were, on the 27th August, borne to Greenside Well, and there burned. The spot of execution was selected so that the flames might be witnessed by, and strike terror among, the people of Fifeshire. Norman Gourlay had denied the existence of purgatory, and affirmed that the Pope was Antichrist.[3]

On the site of Melbourne Place, at Edinburgh, stood a large mansion known as Robert Gourlay's house, and having over the principal entrance the legend : " O Lord in thé is al my traist, 1569." Robert Gourlay, the original owner, was a messenger-at-arms connected with Holyrood Abbey, an office bestowed upon him by the commendator, Adam Bothwell, Bishop of Orkney. An

---

[1] Exchequer Rolls, vol. i., 620.
[2] Rotuli Scotiæ, vol. i., 897, a b.

[3] Calderwood's History of the Church, i., 104-107.

elder of the church, he was, in May 1574, ordained to profess his repentance in St Giles' Church " for transporting wheat out of the countrie."[1] When, in 1581, about to suffer death, the Regent Morton was for two days detained in Robert Gourlay's house under a strong guard ;[2] and there ensued those remarkable conferences between him and certain ministers, in which, while protesting his innocence of Darnley's murder, he admitted his foreknowledge of it.

John, the eldest son of Robert Gourlay, erected a house at the foot of the alley which conducted to his father's mansion, and in this structure was the Bank of Scotland accommodated from its establishment in 1695 till the year 1805.

On the 8th August 1588, David Gourlay, described as a son of Robert Gourlay, merchant-burgess of Edinburgh, entered into a contract of marriage with Marion, daughter of Robert Primrose, chirurgeon-burgess of Edinburgh. To this contract are named as approvers, on the part of David, his father and mother, Robert Gourlay and Helen Cuik, also his brother John. And he becomes bound to infeft his future wife in an annual-rent of £80 out of the lands of Elryk Myrick, in Balnagowan, Wigtonshire.[3]

On the 2d December 1627, David Gourlay, son of the deceased David Gourlay, merchant-burgess of Edin-

---

[1] Calderwood's History of the Church, ii., 328.

[2] *Ibid.*, iii., 556.

[3] Register of Deeds, vol. xxx., fol. 343.

burgh, granted an obligation to Allan Lockhart, brother-german to the laird of Cleghorn, for the sum of £1000.[1]

At Linlithgow, on the 17th May 1606, Gilbert Gourlay, in Redheuch, entered into a contract for the marriage of Jean Gourlay, daughter of his late brother Michael Gourlay, with Alexander Glen, son of the late John Glen of Inneraven, in Fife. A witness to the contract is Patrick Gourlay, portioner of Redheuch.[2]

James Gourlay, portioner of Dalkeith, granted in October 1638 an obligation to Mr John Oswald, minister at Pencaitland, for 100 merks.[3]

John Gourlay of Rowlwood, in Roxburghshire, is named upon an inquest, expede on the 15th February 1497-8.[4] At Jedburgh, on the 20th June 1640, John Gourlay of Rowlwood engaged in a contract with William Turnbull, in Hassendenebank, as to the payment of an annual-rent out of his lands of Rowlwood.[5]

[1] Register of Deeds, vol. xxx., fol. 348.
[2] *Ibid.*
[3] *Ibid.*

[4] Historical Commissioners' Report, vii., Appendix 729.
[5] Fife Register of Sasines, vol. 84.

———o———

FAMILIES IN FIFESHIRE.

Families in Fifeshire.

Gourlay of Kincraig.

Hugh de Gourlay, grandson of Ingelram de Gurley, the original settler in Scotland, held lands in the Lothians, and in Fifeshire.[1] Dying early in the reign of Alexander II., he was in his lands succeeded by his son Hugh. This gentleman made a donation to the Monastery of Newbottle. In the charter or gift, he is designed "Hugo de Gourlay, filius Hugonis."[2] In 1272 he is witness to a confirmation by Bishop William Wishart of St Andrews of the churches of Innerwyc and Lygerwod.[3] He died early in the reign of Alexander III., leaving two sons, William and Hugh.

Hugh de Gourlay, the second son, became steward to the Earl of Dunbar. As witness to a donation to the monks of Coldingham in 1261, he is designed "Hugo de Gourlay, senescallus comitis de Dunbar."[4]

William de Gourlay, elder son of Hugh, succeeded to the family estates. He is named in a donation to the Monastery of Newbottle. He died prior to 1290, leaving a son William.

William acquired lands in different localities. To the Monastery of Newbottle he granted certain lands

[1] See *supra*.
[2] Chartulary of Newbottle, p. 91.
[3] Chartulary of Paisley.
[4] Writs of Coldingham, p. 58.

lying near Arthur's Oon, in the county of Stirling. In the charter, which is dated 2d July 1293, he is designed " Willielmus de Gourlay, filius et hæres Willielmi de Gourlay." [1] He died in the reign of King Robert the Bruce, and was in his lands succeeded by his son Simon de Gourlay, who became coroner of Fife.

Simon de Gourlay of Kincraig married Elizabeth, daughter and heiress of John Alderston of that ilk. In the year 1345 she conveyed the barony of Alderston to her husband, reserving her liferent. Simon de Gourlay annexed the estate of Alderston to his barony of Kincraig. He had two sons, John and William. John, the elder son, died young and unmarried.

William, the second son, succeeded to the family estate. He died towards the close of the reign of David II., leaving two sons, John and William.

John of Kincraig, the elder son, married a daughter of Sir Walter Bickerton of Luffness or Aberlady, a notable baron in the reign of Robert III. [2] Dying without surviving issue, he was succeeded by his brother William, who, being of extravagant habits, alienated a portion of the family estate. He was father of Alexander Gourlay, who in 1394 obtained a warrant from Robert III. " for recognoscing in his Majesty's hands, some acres of land in the barony of Kincraig, which his father had mortified to the church

<hr>

[1] Chartulary of Newbottle, p. 96.   [2] Nisbet's Heraldry, vol. i., p. 349.

of St Monance, without the consent of the Superior."[1] Alexander Gourlay married a daughter of ——— Lauder of Balcomie,[2] by whom he had a son, John, who, on the 30th July 1431, was served heir to his father in the lands of Alderston, Plewlands, Caponflat, and others, in the constabulary of Haddington.[3] In 1457, John Gourlay of Kincraig witnesses the rectification of the boundaries of Kinghorn, Wester and Easter; also in 1466, the rectification of the lands of Gaytmilk (Goatmilk), in the parish of Kinglassie. He died in the reign of James II., and was succeeded by his son, John Gourlay, who in 1443 married Elizabeth, daughter of James Abercrombie of Balcormo.[4] Upon his father's resignation, John Gourlay, on the 28th April 1444, received from James, Bishop of St Andrews, a charter of the lands of Innergelly and others. He had two sons, John and Alexander.

Alexander, the second son, was by his brother John, on the 7th January 1467, appointed bailie of his barony of Alderston.[5]

John, the elder son, succeeded to Kincraig. As "John Gourlay of Kincraig," he is named on an inquest which, on the 19th May 1489, found that Sir Norman Leslie was heir of the late Sir David of

---

[1] Warrant in possession of the family.

[2] Wood's East Neuk of Fife, pp. 37, 258.

[3] Retour in possession of the family.

[4] Marriage Contract in possession of the family.

[5] Family Papers.

Leslie, in the barony of Balinbreck.[1] He married
Margaret, daughter of ——— Monypenny of Pitmilly,
and by her had a son, Alexander.

On the 14th May 1491, Alexander Gourlay had
confirmed to him a charter, whereby his grandfather,
John Gourlay of Kincraig, conveyed to him the lands
of Alderston and others.[2] On the 14th May 1492, he
had a charter under the Great Seal of the lands of
Alderston, Reddercraig, and others; and in 1495 he
had sasine of the lands of Kincraig.[3] On the 7th July
1511, James IV. granted to Alexander Gourlay of Kincraig and his heirs, three-eighth parts of Uchtirmairnie,
in the territory of Kennochy (Kennoway), which lands
were lately adjudged to be in the King's hands.[4]

Alexander Gourlay of Kincraig married Helen,
daughter of John Cockburn of Ormiston, by whom he
had a son, William; also a daughter, Margaret.

Margaret Gourlay married Patrick Blackadder of
Dundaff; they had, on the 13th April 1542, a charter
of the lands of Dundaff.

William Gourlay had, on the 26th August 1538, a
charter of half the lands of Kincraig, and of Auchter-
mairnie and others, which he had resigned into the
King's hands.[5] By another charter under the Great
Seal, dated the 12th June 1540, he and his wife, Janet

---

[1] Fourth Report of Historical Commissioners: Rothes Family Papers, app. 503.

[2] Register of the Great Seal, book xii.,
No. 370.

[3] Exchequer Rolls, vol. x.

[4] Register of the Great Seal, book xvii.,
No. 58.

[5] *Ibid*, book xxvi., No. 111.

Forman, received half the lands of Kincraig; also the lands of Alderston, Caponflat, Plewlands, Pethdales, and others, in the constabulary of Haddington, which the King incorporated into the free barony of Kincraig.[1]

William Gourlay of Kincraig married, secondly, Janet Kellie; he died in or prior to 1560.[2]

In the barony of Kincraig, William Gourlay was succeeded by his son, Alexander. On the 6th August 1579, James VI. confirmed a charter whereby William Lundy, of that ilk, granted to Alexander Gourlay half the lands of Kincraig.[3]

Alexander Gourlay of Kincraig married Janet, daughter of Thomas Scott of Abbotshall, who survived him, and died before 1607. Of the marriage were born two sons, Thomas and William. William, the second son, married Elizabeth Balfour.[4]

Dying about the year 1600, Alexander Gourlay was succeeded by Thomas, his eldest son. On the 17th July 1600, Thomas Gourlay had under the Great Seal confirmed to him the lands of Gordonshall, which he had purchased from John Borthwick of Balhouflie.[5] Thomas Gourlay married Barbara, daughter of Robert Paterson of Dunmure. Under the Great Seal, he and his wife had, on the 15th February 1587, a charter of the lands and barony of Kincraig.

---

[1] Register of the Great Seal, book xxviii., No. 17.

[2] Wood's East Neuk of Fife, p. 258.

[3] Reg. Great Seal, book xxxv., No. 80.

[4] Wood's East Nuke of Fife, p. 258.

[5] Register of the Great Seal, book xlii., No. 70.

Thomas Gourlay of Kincraig died in February 1627 ; and his testament-dative was, on the 14th of the following March, given up by David Brown of Finmonth as a creditor.[1]

By his wife, Barbara Paterson, Thomas Gourlay had a son, William.

William Gourlay, son of Thomas Gourlay, married Jean, daughter of James Macgill of Nether Rankeillor ; their Marriage Contract is dated 1st April 1609. William predeceased his father, leaving a son, Thomas ; also a daughter, Janet, who married William Duddingston of Sandford.[2]

From his grandfather, Thomas Gourlay of Kincraig, Thomas, son of William, had, on the 29th May 1612, a charter of "the sunny half of Kincraig."[3] In 1631, Thomas succeeded to the barony. He was, as one of the Committee of Parliament in 1644, ardently attached to the cause of Charles I. At the Restoration, he, in reward of service, received the honour of knighthood. A member of the Archery Company of St Andrews, he was winner at the competition in 1642, and consequently had the privilege of attaching a silver medal, inscribed with his name and arms, to one of the Company's silver arrows. The arrow, with two others, bearing seventy-nine medals, is preserved at St Andrews in the Museum of the United College. As

[1] St Andrew's Com. Reg.
[2] Wood's East Neuk of Fife, p. 258.
[3] Register of the Great Seal, book xlvii., No. 104.

"Sir Thomas Gourlay of Kincraig, Knight," he had, on the 19th September 1653, sasine of a mansion and portion of ground at Elie.[1] He was a Commissioner of Supply for Fife and Kinross in 1655, 1656, and 1659.[2] He died about 1670.

Sir Thomas Gourlay married Janet, daughter of Robert Bruce of Pitlogie,[3] by whom he had two sons, Thomas and John; also two daughters, Jane and Margaret.

Jane, elder daughter, married, 26th June 1656, Robert Lentrone, Provost of St Andrews, with issue a son, James, baptized 23d April 1657.[4]

Margaret, second daughter, was baptized on the 12th March 1642.[5] She married, 28th December 1665, Nathaniel Spens of Lathallan;[6] a sasine proceeding on their marriage contract is dated 3d November 1665.[7] On the 3d March 1670, she received, in liferent, a charter of the east half of the lands of Lathallan, on her husband's resignation.[8] She had a son, Thomas.[9]

John, younger son of Sir Thomas Gourlay, studied medicine, first at Edinburgh, and afterwards in Paris; he thereafter practised as a physician at Elie, in Fife. In 1660 he married Margaret, daughter of Dr Sharp,

[1] Fife Register of Sasines, vol. xviii., fol. 361.

[2] Acta Parl. Scot., VI., Part ii., 847.

[3] Fife Register of Sasines, vol. ix., fol. 168, 169.

[4] Kilconquhar Parish Register.

[5] *Ibid.*

[6] Kilconquhar Parish Register.

[7] Fife Register of Sasines, new series, vol. iii.

[8] Register of the Great Seal, book lxv. No. 88.

[9] *Ibid.*

physician in Edinburgh.[1] On the occasion of his marriage, he received from his father a small portion of the Alderston estate.[2] He died in 1667, leaving two daughters, Margaret and Helen.[3]

Thomas, the elder son, died in 1661, predeceasing his father. He married, 24th July 1657, Margaret, daughter of William Forbes, younger of Rires, by whom he had three sons; also a daughter, Margaret, who married first, her cousin, Thomas Spens of Lathallan; and secondly, the Rev. Hew Kemp, minister at Dunfermline.

Of the three sons of Thomas Gourlay and Margaret Forbes, Arthur, born posthumously, and baptized 1st March 1662,[4] died young.

Thomas, the eldest son, baptized 8th October 1658,[5] succeeded his grandfather in the barony of Kincraig. Of remarkable strength, no one might venture to wrestle with him; and when the mansion of Kincraig was being erected, and a lintel gave way, he sustained the weight on his shoulders till a support was provided.[6] He died in April 1683, unmarried.[7]

William Gourlay, second son of Thomas Gourlay and Margaret Forbes, was baptized 17th January 1660.[8] In 1683 he succeeded his brother in the barony of Kincraig,

---

[1] Wood's East Neuk of Fife, pp. 173, 258.

[2] Fife Reg. of Sasines, new series, vol. i.

[3] Wood's East Neuk of Fife, p. 528.

[4] Kilconquhar Parish Register.

[5] Kilconquhar Parish Register.

[6] Wood's East Neuk of Fife, p. 258.

[7] Fife Register of Sasines, 27th May 1683.

[8] Kilconquhar Parish Register.

and died in December 1718.[1] He married Jean, only child of John Lessells, Provost of Haddington. He had three sons—Thomas, William, and John ; also three daughters.

Janet, the eldest daughter, married Captain Reid of the Dragoons, with issue a daughter, who married —— Ker of Cavers.

Helen, second daughter, died unmarried.

Jean, third daughter, married Dr John Scott of Coats.

Of the sons, Thomas, the eldest, predeceased his father.

William, second son, succeeded to Kincraig, and died in 1776.[2] He married a daughter of George Seton of Pitmedden (who died in 1792), with issue a son, George, and a daughter, Mary Anne.

Mary Anne Gourlay married Dr Tait, surgeon in Elie, and died in 1776, without issue.[3]

George Gourlay, younger of Kincraig, married in 1757 Margaret, only child of William Robertson, of the family of Bedlay, Writer to the Signet. He predeceased his father, dying prior to the 14th January 1774, when his testament-dative was given up by his son William, and his daughters Margaret and Mary.[4]

William, only son of George Gourlay, succeeded to

[1] St Andrews Com. Reg., 14th November 1719.

[2] *Ibid.*, 24th May 1777.

[3] Wood's East Neuk of Fife, p. 259.

[4] St Andrews Com. Reg., 14th January 1774.

D

the barony of Kincraig on the death of his grandfather in 1776.[1] In 1792 he died unmarried.

John, third son of William Gourlay and Jean Lessells, settled in Haddington as a wine merchant. He married Elizabeth, daughter of David Plenderleath of Kailzie, by whom he had a son, William. This gentleman some time practised as a physician in Madeira, and in 1792 succeeded his cousin William in the barony of Kincraig. He died on the 18th November 1827, aged sixty-six. He is commemorated on a mural tablet at the family burying-place in Kilconquhar churchyard.

William Gourlay of Kincraig married first, in 1787, Catherine, daughter of Colonel Philip Van Cortlandt, of America, by whom he had a son, John; also four daughters.

John Gourlay, who succeeded his father in the barony of Kincraig, died in December 1833 unmarried, and was in the lands succeeded by his cousin Margaret Gourlay, daughter of George, and grand-daughter of William, of Kincraig. She died in 1846 unmarried, and was succeeded by her cousin, Catherine, eldest daughter of William Gourlay of Kincraig.

Catherine Gourlay, latterly of Kincraig, married, first, Captain Roden Douglas, Royal Navy, and, secondly, James Bean, of Madeira. She died in December 1864.

Elizabeth, second daughter of William Gourlay of Kincraig, died unmarried.

[1] St Andrews Com. Reg., 24th May 1777.

Gertrude, fourth daughter, died unmarried.

Jean Plenderleath, third daughter, married John Austin, General in the Portuguese service, and settled in Madeira. She died in 1823, leaving a son and three daughters.

William Edmund Craufurd Austin, only son of General Austin and Jean Plenderleath Gourlay, born in 1821, succeeded his aunt, Catherine Gourlay, as proprietor of Kincraig, when he assumed the additional name of Gourlay. He is M.A., and Rector of Stanton St John, Oxfordshire. He married in 1863 Emily, daughter of Captain Frederick Blair, R.N., without issue.

Elizabeth Page, eldest daughter of General Austin, by his wife Jean Plenderleath Gourlay, died in 1879 unmarried.

Susan Arbuthnot Craufurd, second daughter, married the Rev. William Gorst Harrison, Rector of Easington, in the county of Durham, with issue a son, Gilbert Eliot, Lieutenant Royal Navy; also nine daughters—Gertrude, Susan, Kathleen, Emily, Julia, Winifred, Rachel, Decima, and Beatrice.

Anna Maria Margaret Catherine, third daughter, married Lieutenant William Charles Callow, who died in 1853.

William Gourlay of Kincraig married secondly, in 1822, Mary, only daughter of James Mackintosh (who died in 1879); she had two daughters. Marion Bean, the elder daughter, died unmarried on the 27th February

1888. Helen, younger daughter, died unmarried on the 30th December 1845.

The family arms, *sable;* an eagle displayed *argent,* armed and beaked *gules.* Crest : such another eagle issuing out of the torss. Motto : *Profunda cernit.*

———o———

ffamilies at Largo, ffalkland, and king's kettle.

In the Revenue Returns for 1486-1492, Thomas Gourlay is, under the "Quarter of Falkland," entered as tenant of the Mill of Aldhall.[1]

In the rental of 1492-1500 of the "Quarter of Largo," James Gourlay appears as tenant of an eighth of Newton Rires.[2] Patrick Gourlay was subsequently tenant at Newton Rires.[3]

In the rental of 1492-1500, John Gourlay is named as tenant of "a fourth of Kettle."[4] At Perth, on the 29th September 1541, James V. granted in feu ferme to John Gourlay, son and heir of the late John Gourlay, a quarter of the land of Katill (Kettle).[5]

On the 23d January 1589, Walter Gourlay, portioner of King's Kettle, executed his will. He appointed his wife, Isobel Lummisdain, as his executrix, and provided

---

[1] Exchequer Rolls, vol. x.
[2] *Ibid.*
[3] Wood's East Neuk of Fife, p. 63.

Newton Rires is now included in the estate of Charleton.
[4] Exchequer Rolls, vol. x.
[5] Register of the Great Seal, xxviii., 548.

that in the event of her second marriage, Walter Heriot of Ramorgany (Ramornie), and Mr Thomas Lummisdain, "persoun of Kinkell," should become tutors to his eldest son.[1]

On the 26th December 1605, Walter Gourlay, son and heir of the deceased Walter Gourlay, portioner of King's Kettle, obtained sasine of the fourth part of the lands of King's Kettle.[2]

————o————

ffamilies at Dysart, Wemyss, Scoonie, Elie, and Anstruther.

At Edinburgh, on the 14th April 1513, Robert Gourlay, burgess of Dysart, and Grissel Wemyss, his spouse, had a charter of the lands of Hauch, on the resignation of Andrew Kynnynmonth.[3]

Magnus Gourlay, burgess of Wester Wemyss, granted, on the 31st August 1622, an obligation to Thomas Alexander of Drumeldrie, for £215.[4]

On the 3d February 1659, Thomas Gourlay, in Scoonie, and Christian Pittillok, his wife, had sasine in a tenement in the sea-town of Largo.[5]

---

[1] St Andrews Com. Register.

[2] Fifeshire Register of Sasines.

[3] Register of Great Seal, xviii., 152.

[4] Register of Deeds, vol. 350.

[5] Fifeshire Register of Sasines, vol. xxi., fol. 23.

Scions of the House of Gourlay of Kincraig had settled at Elie, in or prior to the seventeenth century. At the baptism of a child of George Gourlay, in Elie, on the 12th June 1672, the laird of Kincraig was a witness.[1] George Gourlay was captain of a coasting vessel, and owner of the eighth of "The Hopewell of Anstruther," and tenth of "The Margaret of Elie." He died in March 1776, when his "free gear" was valued at £2467, 6s. 8d. He bequeathed £100 for "a handsome burial stane to be placed abune his corps;" and made provision that in the failure of his own children, his substance should be inherited by the children of his brother John, skipper or ship-captain in Anstruther.[2]

At Elie, on the west of Auchmuty's Wynd, and close to the sea, a large house of castellated form, and evidently built in the sixteenth century, was the property of the Kincraig family. It was probably used as a marine residence.[3]

---

[1] Elie Parish Register. [2] St Andrews Com. Reg., May 2, 1676.
[3] Wood's East Neuk of Fife, p. 66.

Family at Dunfermline.

To a Precept by Archbishop James Beaton of St Andrews, for the induction of Sir Walter Stewart to the parish church of St Ninian's of Kirktown, dated at the Abbey of Dunfermline 10th November 1527, Alexander Gourlay is a witness.[1]

At Torry, on the 7th April 1542, a charter of sale was granted by Henry Stewart of Rossyth to Margaret Gourlay, lady of Torry, in liferent, and to Patrick Blacater, her son, in fee, of the lands of Dunduff, in the barony of Rossyth. One of the witnesses is James Gourlay.[2]

To a Precept of Sasine, dated at Dunfermline 3d March 1544, Thomas Gourlay is a witness. Thomas Gourlay and his wife had, about the year 1555, a charter of feu ferme of the seventeenth part of Over Grange of South Ferry.[3]

Between the years 1555 and 1583, William Durie and Jeanne Gourlay, his wife, had a charter of feu ferme of a fourth part of the lands of Newlands; they had also a charter of the lands of Kelty.[4] On the 7th June 1566, Robert, Archdean of St Andrews, granted to William Durie and Jean Gourlay, his wife, in free tenement, a charter of the lands of Medo-end, in the regality of Dunfermline.[5]

[1] Chartulary of Cambuskenneth, p. 157.
[2] Register of Great Seal, xxviii., 178.
[3] Register of Dunfermline.
[4] Ibid.
[5] Register of Great Seal, xxxiii., 13.

Family at Kinghorn.

About the year 1555 John Gourlay of Kincraig received "an assedation" of the eighteenth part of Over Grange of Kinghorn Wester.[1]

On the 16th November 1619, Archibald Gourlay, burgess of Kinghorn, executed his Will; he appointed as his executrix his wife, Elspeth Glen.[2]

George Gourlay, skipper-burgess of Kinghorn, and his wife, Marion Cunningham, had in December 1646 sasine of eighty merks out of tenements of land called Killeraik of Kinghorn.[3]

On the 18th June 1706, William Gourlay, burgess of Kinghorn, received from William Edmond an obligation for £70.[4]

[1] Register of Dunfermline.
[2] St Andrews Commissariot Register.
[3] Fifeshire Register of Sasines.
[4] Register of Deeds, vol. cxxxii., May 11, 1707.

ffamilies in Ceres.

A branch of the family of Kincraig settled in the parish of Ceres early in the seventeenth century. On the 18th May 1629, Thomas Mortoun at Pitscottie, a deacon of the parish church of Ceres, and his wife Margaret Gourlay, had a child baptized, one of the witnesses being Sir John Hope of Craighall.[1]

On the 7th October 1674, Thomas Gourlay, tenant in Baldirran, parish of Ceres, received sasine of an annual-rent of £80 out of the lands of Baltullie and the lands of Kirkland.[2] His testament-dative was on the 19th February 1683 given up by his widow, on behalf of Thomas Gourlay, their only son,—his free gear being valued at £959, 1s. 8d.[3]

John Gourlay, farmer in Kinninmonth, parish of Ceres, died in December 1695. In his inventory, given up by his widow, his "free gear" is valued at £369.[4] John Gourlay married, in June 1674, Elizabeth Carstares, of the parish of Kilconquhar.[5] His son John, farmer at Denhead in the parish of Ceres, died prior to the 10th November 1723.[6]

John Gourlay, farmer at Denhead, had by his wife,

[1] Ceres Parish Register.
[2] Fifeshire Register of Sasines.
[3] St Andrews Com. Register.
[4] *Ibid.*
[5] Ceres Parish Register. Elizabeth

Carstares was a member of the landed family of Carstares of Kilconquhar, to which belonged the celebrated Principal Carstares of Edinburgh.
[6] Ceres Parish Register.

Helen Black, an eldest son Robert, who was born 27th October 1704.[1] He succeeded to his father's lease of Denhead farm, and on the 14th November 1737 received in feu the mill lands of Craigrothie.[2] He married Barbara, daughter of William Beath, residing at Kilmuck, parish of Scoonie, and by her had four sons, William, John, Oliver, and David.[3]

Oliver, the third son, was baptized on the 18th August 1740. Having some years engaged in legal pursuits at Edinburgh, he returned to his native county. In April 1774 he had sasine of the lands of Newton Leys, Bonnybanks, Newbigging, and others, in the parish of Ceres; and in April 1779 he obtained the lands of Balhilly, Craigrothie Mill, and the Mains of Scotstarvet.[4]

In acquiring these and other lands, Oliver Gourlay was led to believe that by a course of high farming he would attain opulence. Ardent in his enterprises, he in 1780 invited the Town Council of St Andrews to construct a superior road between their city and his estate, assuring them that thereby they "would eternize their names."[5] Impressed by his agricultural activities, capitalists extended to him a large credit, so that prior to 1803 he was enabled to purchase the estate of Kilmaron, near Cupar-Fife, of which the modern

---

[1] Ceres Parish Register.
[2] Fifeshire Register of Sasines.
[3] Ceres Parish Register.
[4] Fifeshire Register of Sasines.
[5] St Andrews Town Council Records.

rental was upwards of £3000.[1] But Mr Gourlay failed in his agricultural adventures, and disposing of his lands, he retired from public concerns. He died on the 10th October 1819 in his eightieth year.[2]

Oliver Gourlay married in 1774 Janet, only daughter of Thomas Fleming, tenant in Nether Friarton ; she died 10th October 1827 at the age of seventy-three.[3] Of the marriage were born two sons, Robert Fleming and Thomas ; also five daughters, Catharine, Barbara, Janet, Helen, and Margaret.[4]

Robert Fleming Gourlay, the elder son, was born on the 24th March 1778.[5] After studying for several sessions at the University of St Andrews, he began a political career by printing a pamphlet on Reform, and covertly distributing copies throughout the county. As his opinions were extreme, and his mode of propagating them obnoxious, it was determined to charge him with sedition. From this difficulty Mr Gourlay made an escape by removing to England and there renting a small farm at Deptford in Kent. Subsequently emigrating to Canada, he there acquired a large tract of land, on which he endeavoured to induce his countrymen to make settlements. On the resources of Canada he published a work in three volumes ; also a number of pamphlets. Returning from America, he made a

[1] Parliamentary Returns—Lands and Heritages, 1874.

[2] Tombstone Inscription in Ceres churchyard.

[3] Tombstone Inscription in Ceres churchyard.

[4] *Ibid.*

[5] Ceres Parish Register.

progress throughout Great Britain setting forth his views on public affairs, more especially on emigration. Having experienced some inattention at the hands of Henry, afterwards Lord Brougham, he in the lobby of the House of Commons attacked him with a horsewhip, an escapade which led to his being sent to prison. During a long career he committed many other extravagances; but in private life he was generous, humane, and circumspect. He died on the 1st August 1863, at the age of eighty-five. In the family burying-ground at Ceres, he has been careful to denote his descent from "Ingelramus Gourlay, who came from England with Prince William about the year 1174."

Robert Fleming Gourlay was twice married, but his race is extinct in the male line.

———0———

Families at St Andrews.

William Gourlay, one of the collectors of customs at St Andrews, rendered his account on the 14th June 1403, also on the 8th July 1404, and on the 22d March 1405-6.[1]

David Gourlay of Southfield, parish of Largo, died on the 8th October 1627.[2] By his second wife, Christian Ramsay, he had two sons, Alexander and Robert.

Alexander, the elder son, succeeded his father in the lands of Southfield, which, on the 29th July 1630, he sold to his brother Robert.[3] On the 13th June 1628, he, on a charter from Archbishop John Spottiswood of St Andrews, had sasine of half the lands of Polduff, otherwise called Smiddiegreen, in the lordship of Byrehills (Boarhills).[4] From Smiddiegreen he, prior to 1636, removed to the farm of Lamboletham, which he took on lease.[5] On the 10th June 1645 he had sasine of a tenement of land at Anstruther.[6]

Alexander Gourlay married Susannah Jardine, by whom he had three sons, Alexander, James, and David ; also three daughters, Margaret, Marjory, and Janet.

---

[1] Exchequer Rolls, vol. iii., p. 571.
[2] St Andrews Com. Register.
[3] Register of Deeds, vol 470.
[4] Fifeshire Register of Sasines, vol. vii., fol. 257.
[5] St Andrews Parish Register.
[6] Fifeshire Register of Sasines, vol. xv.

At the baptism of Alexander, the eldest son, on the 27th September 1629, the Archdean of St Andrews was a witness.[1]

To Thomas Gourlay, advocate in St Andrews, and his wife, Margaret Clephane, Sir Alexander Drummond of Gibliston granted a bond for 500 merks ; it is dated at St Andrews 5th November 1629.[2]

On the 29th June 1649, David Gourlay, son and heir of the late David Gourlay, citizen of St Andrews, obtained sasine on a precept from Chancery, as heir to his father, in nine acres and two roods of arable land in the neighbourhood of the burgh.[3]

To Walter Gourlay and his wife, Bessie Watson, at St Andrews, was baptized, on the 18th April 1628, a son, Robert.[4] Robert settled as a trader in his native city. He married Margaret Dishart, by whom he had three sons, William, James, and John.[5]

John, the third and youngest son, was baptized on the 27th August 1667.[6] Conducting business as a manufacturer in St Andrews, he attained a measure of opulence. By his wife, Agnes Miller, he had a son, Robert.

Robert Gourlay, son of John Gourlay and Agnes Miller, was born on the 28th September 1707. Obtaining a share of, and ultimately succeeding to, his father's

---

[1] St Andrews Parish Register.

[2] Register of Deeds, vol. 498.

[3] Fifeshire Register of Sasines, vol. xi., fol. 122.

[4] St Andrews Parish Register.

[5] *Ibid.*

[6] *Ibid.*

business, he was, prior to 1748, elected Deacon of his craft. He also became clerk to the Kirk Session of St Leonard's parish.[1] He died on the 18th February 1791 at the age of eighty-four.[2]

Robert Gourlay married Anna Brown, by whom he had three sons, John, Robert, and Charles.[3] Robert, second son, born 30th May 1751, settled in St Andrews as a merchant, and was in 1792 elected Convener of the Incorporated Trades.[4] He died at St Andrews on the 1st of September 1811 at the age of sixty.[5] By his wife, Agnes Liddell, he had six sons—Robert, John, Charles, John Brown, Thomas, and James; also two daughters.[6]

Agnes Cree, elder daughter, born 29th November 1786, married in 1807 Alexander Kay, with issue.

Anne, younger daughter, born 4th March 1796, married Francis Hamilton, with issue.

Of the sons, Robert, born 18th January 1789, married Janet Marshall, of Chapelton, Lanarkshire; he died in 1852, without issue. John died in infancy. Charles, born 1st December 1792, died in 1863 unmarried.

John Brown, born 12th September 1799, settled in Glasgow, and there died in 1878. By his wife, Sarah Langlands, who died in 1887, he had three sons and four daughters—(1.) Robert, eldest son, born in 1825, is a

---

[1] St Andrews Parish Register.

[2] St Andrews Deaths' Register. On his tombstone in St Andrews churchyard, the sculptor has erroneously described his age as fifty-four.

[3] St Andrews Parish Register.

[4] *Ibid.*

[5] St Andrews Deaths' Register. Tombstone Inscription.

[6] St Andrews Parish Register.

merchant in Glasgow; he married his cousin Agnes Gourlay, with issue two sons, John, born 27th May 1867, and Robert James, born 26th February 1873; also four daughters, Jane, Sarah, Agnes (deceased), and Annie: (2.) William, second son, born in 1827, settled in London, married Margaret Finlay, without issue: (3.) John, third son, born in 1836, is a chartered accountant in Glasgow; he married Elizabeth Nash, only daughter of the Rev. Andrew Murray, with issue seven sons—John George, born in 1870, died in infancy; Andrew Murray, born in 1871; William Robert, born in 1874; Charles Aikman, born in 1877; Henry, born in 1880; James Nash, born in 1881; John Brown, born in 1884, died in infancy; also two daughters—Elizabeth Nash, born in 1872, died in infancy; and Sarah Langlands, born in 1876.

Of the four daughters of John Brown Gourlay, Margaret, born in 1829, and Sarah, born in 1834, are unmarried. Agnes, third daughter, born in 1838, married Charles B. Aikman, solicitor in Glasgow, without issue. Isabella, fourth daughter, born in 1842, married Thomas Clark, Largs, with issue a son.

Thomas, fifth son of Robert Gourlay and Agnes Liddell, born 16th October 1802, died young and unmarried.

James, youngest son of Robert Gourlay, born at St Andrews on the 3d June 1804, was one of the leading accountants in Glasgow. After retiring from business, he in 1855 accepted an agency for the Bank of Scotland at Laurieston in the same city. A magistrate of

Glasgow, he was a chief promoter of the Loch Katrine Water Scheme. He died in May 1877. In 1830 he married Jeanie Cleland (who died in September 1870), with issue, one son and four daughters.

Agnes, the eldest daughter, born 15th December 1833, married, in 1859, her cousin, Robert Gourlay, with issue.

Jane, second daughter, born in February 1836, died in 1886, unmarried.

Annie, third daughter, born 26th April 1838, married, in 1861, Henry Shaw Macpherson, merchant in Glasgow, with issue.

Helen, fourth and youngest daughter, born 6th April 1843, is unmarried.

Robert, only son of James Gourlay and Jeanie Cleland, born 13th July 1840, is manager of the Bank of Scotland, Glasgow, and a magistrate of the County of Lanark. He married in March 1868, Mary Brown Hastings Moffat, Gateside, Kirkconnel, Dumfriesshire, who died 17th December 1877. Of the marriage were born three sons: James, born 1869; Robert Cleland, born 1871; Francis Nicholson Moffat, born 1872; also two daughters, Agnes Jessie and Mary Moffat, both of whom died in infancy.

———o———

FAMILIES IN LANARKSHIRE
STIRLINGSHIRE AND PERTHSHIRE

Families in Lanarkshire.

On the 19th July 1576, James VI. confirmed a charter whereby, on the 3d May 1561, Mr Arthur Hamilton, provost of the Collegiate Church of Hamilton, granted to Robert Gourlaw, familiar servitor of James, Duke of Chatelherault, a tenement of land, with houses, hedges, fruit-trees, etc., in the town of Hamilton,—also ten acres of land in Hamilton-hauch, in the barony of Hamilton.[1]

William Gourlie, the eminent botanist, was born at Glasgow in March 1815, and died on the 24th June 1856.

Robert Gourlaw, a native of Lanarkshire, was, on the 31st March 1692, ordained minister of Tillicoultry ; he died in 1713.[2]

[1] Register of Great Seal, xxxiv., 636.   [2] Fasti Eccl. Scot., ii., 740.

Families in Stirlingshire.

At Clackmannan, on the 13th June 1330, Robert Gourlay, provost of Stirling, rendered to the chamberlain his accounts for that burgh.[1]

John Gourlay is, on the 28th February 1388-9, named as a landowner at Stirling.[2]

At Perth, on the 20th March 1465-6, John Gourlay, one of the bailies of Stirling, rendered his account for that burgh.[3]

On the 25th September 1479, John Gourlay is named as possessing lands at Stirling.[4]

The late David Gurlay, owner of "two riggis," is named in a charter subscribed at Stirling on the 7th February 1525-6.[5]

On the 3d March 1642, a charter under the Great Seal was granted to Robert Gourlay in Patrickstown of Lecky, in life-rent, and to Robert Gourlay, younger, his son, of the lands of Offerance of Lecky, commonly called Schyrgartoun, in the Stewartry of Menteith, on the resignation of Alexander Lecky of that Ilk.[6]

In the year 1666 Robert Gourlay of Little Kerse is named; also his wife Bethia, daughter of Walter Graham of Meiklewood.[7]

[1] Exchequer Rolls, i., 266.
[2] Stirling Burgh Charters, p. 23.
[3] Exchequer Rolls, iii., 637.
[4] Stirling Burgh Records.
[5] Stirling Burgh Charters, pp. 193, 194.
[6] Register of the Great Seal, lvii., 13.
[7] Stirlingshire Com. Reg., vol. vii.

On the 2d July 1670, Robert Gourlay, eldest son of Robert Gourlay of Little Kerse, called Shirgarton, is named in a sasine, with reference to the lands of Kipdarroch in the parish of Gargunnock.[1]

On the 16th and 21st November 1768, David Gourlay of Kipdarroch received a disposition of the lands of Easter and Wester Callichat.[2]

On the 9th May 1761, Mr James Gourlay, Preacher of the Gospel, son of Archibald Gourlay of Birkhill, near Stirling, granted a disposition of these lands in favour of George Muschet, merchant, Stirling.[3] Licensed by the Presbytery of Glasgow on the 2d August 1758, he was ordained minister of Tillicoultry on the 25th September 1765. In 1772 he demitted his charge, and went to America.[4]

Hugh Gourlay, licensed by the Presbytery of Stirling on the 26th April 1760, was ordained minister of Balfron on the 25th September of the same year. He died on the 11th January 1787, aged fifty-five. He married, first, Margaret Lauder; secondly, 30th July 1782, Elizabeth Colquhoun, with issue.

---

[1] Stirlingshire Register of Sasines, 2d series, vol. iv., fol. 186.

[2] *Ibid.*, vol. xxiii., fol. 175.

[3] Stirlingshire Register of Sasines, 2d series, vol. xxiv., fol. 465.

[4] Fasti Eccl. Scot., ii., 711.

Families in Perthshire.

On the 19th December 1521, John Blackadder, fiar of Tulliallan, and Mr Patrick Blackadder, Archdean of Glasgow, granted a charter to Alexander Livingston of Dunipace, and Alison Gourlay, his spouse, in liferent, and to Mr Alexander Livingston, their son, heritably, of the lands of the Overtoun of Tulliallan.[1]

To a charter, granted on the 1st October 1527, by Sir Andrew Murray of Balvaird, to the Abbey of Cambuskenneth, of an annual-rent of fourteen merks, from the lands of Arngrosk (Arngask), Alexander Gourlay is a witness.[2]

By the Regent Mary of Guise was, on the 7th August 1546, confirmed a charter, whereby William, Lord Crichton of Sanquhar, granted to Thomas Gourlaw of Ballendene, the fourth part of Ballendene, in the barony of Balledgarno, and shire of Perth.[3] On the 8th June 1556, the Queen Regent confirmed a charter, in which Thomas Gourlaw of Ballendene grants to Alexander Gourlaw, his son, the fourth part of Ballendene.[4]

At Culross, on the 18th June 1620, Gilbert Gourlay of Wester Grange, in the Lordship of Culross, gave in loan to John Gaw of Maw the sum of 3000 merks, for which he received an annual-rent out of the lands

[1] Register of the Great Seal, xxii., 42.
[2] Register of Cambuskenneth, p. 38.
[3] Register of the Great Seal, xxix., 370.
[4] *Ibid.*, xxx., 491.

of Wester Rothe Wallis.[1] On the 31st May 1637, Gilbert Gourlay of Wester Grange received from Andrew Brand, maltster-burgess of Culross, a bond for two hundred merks.[2] In 1646 Gilbert Gourlay of Wester Grange was placed on the Committee of War for Perthshire.[3]

On the 28th April 1724, Archibald Gourlay received a disposition from William Govan, of the lands of Wester Carse of Boquhaple, in the parish of Kincardine-in-Menteith.[4]

Robert Gourlay of Wester Boquhaple had, on the 12th February 1743, a charter of the lands of Brae in Menteith.[5]

---

[1] Register of Deeds, vol. 310.
[2] *Ibid.*, vol. 506.
[3] Acta Parl. Scot., vol. vi., Pt. 1, p. 622.

[4] Register of the Great Seal, xc., 122.
[5] *Ibid.*, xcvii., 286

———o———

FAMILIES IN THE
NORTHERN COUNTIES

Families in the Northern Counties.

Henry de Gorlay was, on the 25th September 1286, appointed on an inquest to inquire into the boundaries of certain pasture lands in the barony of Panmure.[1] And as Henry de Gorlay, knight, he is put on a commission, appointed on the 14th October 1286.[2]

William de Gourlay de Balgally did homage to Edward I. at Berwick in 1296.[3]

In 1328, William Gourlay is one of the witnesses to a charter, whereby Walter de Schaklock granted to Henry de Ross a third part of the lands of Iniency, near Montrose.[4]

Sir John Gourlay, monk of Aberbrothock, is witness to a citation by John of Eglyntoun, Prior of Blantyre, dated at St Andrews, 28th January 1392; he is also witness to a sentence of excommunication against Robert, bishop of Dunkeld, on the 25th February of the same year.[5]

[1] Harleian Charter, 43, B. 9.

[2] Register of Aberbrothock, 383.

[3] Ragman Roll, 126; Prynne, 654; Palgrave, 196. There are two considerable estates called Balgally, Balgillie, or Balgillo, in the County of Forfar, one of which is situated within the parish and thanedom of Tannadice, the other in the parish of Monifieth (Jervise's "Angus and Mearns," p. 313).

[4] Register of Aberbrothock, 339.

[5] Register of Cambuskenneth, pp. 99, 100, 105.

On the 6th November 1516, James Gurlay (Gourlay) rented from the Abbot of Cupar three acres and three roods of land.[1] In 1558, William Gourlay was tenant of Causeyend, on the lands of the Abbey.[2]

On the 26th January 1600, William Gourlay, described as portioner of Calseyend of Cupar, sold to Charles Bell for £2000, four acres of land at Keithock.[3]

At Dundee, on the 12th November 1602, Thomas Gourlay of Dargo granted to Patrick Cadzow, portioner at Liff, a bond for fifty-five merks.[4] Thomas Gourlay is, in November 1613, named as meal-maker at Invergowrie, in a bond granted by him for 500 merks.[5]

In May 1628, Walter Gourlay, maltster-burgess of Dundee, executed his Will. To his elder son, James, he bequeathed a third part of his estate; and he provided legacies to his son John, and his daughters, Margaret, Jean, and Catherine. His will was confirmed at Brechin in June 1628, when his " free gear " was estimated at £2886, 13s. 4d.[6]

James Gourlay, brother of Walter, died at Dundee in February 1631; his testament-dative was given up by Katherine Alexander, his relict, in name of Walter Gourlay their son.[7]

[1] Rental Book of Abbey of Cupar, vol. i., pp. 291, 292, 312.
[2] *Ibid.*, vol. ii., pp. 74, 75, 170, 183, 213.
[3] Register of Deeds.
[4] Register of Deeds.
[5] *Ibid.*
[6] Brechin Com. Register.
[7] *Ibid.*

Patrick Gourlay in Bervie, died in May 1640, leaving a son, Thomas.[1]

In fortifying the place against the approach of Cromwell, the Magistrates of Dundee removed a tenement belonging to David Gourlay, a burgess, who, failing to obtain compensation, presented a complaint to Parliament. On the 23d June 1649, the Estates ordained the Magistrates to pay to their petitioner the sum of a thousand merks.[2]

Patrick Gourlay, Town Clerk of Dundee, died in January 1667, at the age of forty-seven. To his memory was reared, in the burying-ground, a monument bearing a commendatory inscription, partly in Latin verse.[3]

James Gourlay, glover in Dundee, had a son William, who, graduating at the University of St Andrews in 1736, was, in October 1742, licensed to preach. On the 6th March 1752, he was ordained minister of Flisk, Fifeshire. He died on the 16th October 1780, at the age of seventy. In the living of Flisk he was succeeded by his son William, who died on the 2d March 1810, at the age of sixty-one.[4]

John Gourlay, a native of Brechin, studied at King's College, Aberdeen, and in July 1799 was ordained assistant minister of Arbuthnot. He was translated

[1] Brechin Com. Register.
[2] Acta Parl. Scot., vi., Part ii., p. 483.
[3] Monuments and Monumental Inscriptions in Scotland, vol. ii., p. 215.
[4] Fasti Eccl. Scot., ii., 494.

to the parish of Lintrathen in 1813, and from thence in 1819 to that of Cortachy. He died on the 27th March 1826. By his wife, Sarah Anne Hunter, he had a son, William.[1]

On the 5th May 1540, in an account of money belonging to the Cathedral of Aberdeen, there appears a balance of 6s. 8d., resting in the hands of Sir John Gurla.[2]

---

[1] Fasti Eccl. Scot., iii., 756, 767.   [2] Chartulary of Aberdeen.

INDEX.

Printed by M'Farlane & Erskine, *Edinburgh.*

www.ingramcontent.com/pod-product-compliance
Lightning Source LLC
Chambersburg PA
CBHW021528090426
42739CB00007B/840